Moments

of

Mindfulness

Polly Fielding

ISBN-13: 978-1497438774

ISBN-10: 1497438772

Also by Polly Fielding:

The 5:2 Diet Made eZy

The 5:2 Vegetarian Diet Made eZy

All You Need For The 5:2 Diet
(Co-authored with Lucy Lonsdale & Emily Hanson)

And This Is My Adopted Daughter

A Mind To Be Free

Crossing The Borderline

Letting Go

Missing Factor

Going In Seine

Cover picture and internal art by Polly Fielding

Moments of Mindfulness

Introduction

Think back to the last time you shopped for groceries.

Can you recall your experience at the checkout, what you saw and heard (besides the robotic announcement: 'Unexpected item in bagging area')? If you didn't use the self-service point, do you remember if the assistant was male or female, the colour of their eyes, whether they had curly or straight hair, how they were dressed, exactly what they said to you..?

How often, when you are having a conversation with someone and they are speaking, are you thinking of what you are going to say next instead of giving them your full attention?

And how many times have you driven some

place and wondered how you actually got there? That's not to suggest that you are a bad driver; it's just that things we do habitually like cleaning our teeth, dressing or everyday household chores frequently get done with our thoughts going off in different directions. Rarely are we completely focused on the task in hand.

We spend a lot of time 'sleepwalking' through our lives. What I mean by that is that, too often, we are trying to multi-task, instead of attending wholeheartedly to one thing at a time, or doing stuff on 'automatic pilot'.

Whilst getting showered in the morning I might be thinking about what I'm going to do later in the day, something I did yesterday or what to wear. That doesn't mean I don't wash properly! It does mean, though, that I am not completely aware of what I am doing.

There have also been many times when I have visited the ladies' toilet (the rest room) in a restaurant and on exiting have mindlessly ended up in the staff kitchen or another toilet, simply because I didn't notice the route I came in by!

Thomas Edison, the inventor of the electric light bulb, once asked several of his long-term employees what they noticed every day walking along the path from the road to his factory. When they had finished telling him everything they had seen around them on that fine spring morning, he was astonished to find that not one of them had mentioned the beautiful flowering cherry tree to one side of the path.

We can get so used to *doing* things that we can actually miss out heavily on *experiencing* them.

If we are being mindful, we are paying attention to what is actually going on, fully aware and awake in this moment. And realistically that's all there is – the Here and Now.

By being present we begin to wake up to the

sensation of really living instead of switching off and disappearing somewhere else with our minds. We aren't in the past or the future but *here*, where it's all happening!

When we are functioning in automatic pilot mode our 'buttons' are more easily pressed. Events, thoughts and feelings can trigger unhelpful patterns of thinking (of which we are only vaguely aware, or perhaps not at all) which can end up with us feeling bad. I speak from personal experience!

Once we have a heightened awareness of our thoughts, feelings and bodily sensations we free ourselves up and give ourselves more choice about how we perceive life at any moment; we can then avoid the negative spirals we slip into that may have caused problems in the past. Being mindful enables us to pause, to give ourselves time and space for reflection. By raising our awareness we develop the ability to respond rather than simply react to people and events. And increased openness to life makes the journey through it way more enjoyable and fulfilling. We make the most of each moment, unlike poor Basil, speaking in the sitcom 'Fawlty Towers': "Zoom! What was that? That was your life, mate. That was quick, do I get another? Sorry mate, that's your lot..."

That's all very well, you might be thinking, but I have so many things to get done and I can't possibly shut out all the thoughts filling my head up. But that's the point – don't even try to.

Take time right now to watch what is going on in your mind whilst you are reading this page. Thoughts will come and go even in this short space of time but that's fine - just notice them passing through like clouds, refrain from making any judgment about them or getting caught up in their content and steer your focus gently back to this experience .

I suggest you read the next bit and then try it out for yourself, closing your eyes if it makes it easier for you. It's a very short exercise, lasting only a few minutes, which has helped me to be mindful and which will, I hope, be helpful to you.

First, be *aware* of and just observe what thoughts are in your mind - watch them; then explore and try to name what you are feeling emotionally (happy, worried, self-critical...) and whether you feel tension in any part of your body – forehead, arms, buttocks...

Now *redirect your focus* to your breath – following its journey from the moment it enters your nostrils, flows down your windpipe and expands your chest and abdomen, to its way out, noting any change in temperature as it exits your nose. If any thoughts crop up whilst you are doing this, just briefly acknowledge rather than dwell on them and then return to your breath.

Finally, scan your entire body, including your posture and facial expression, and then *breathe into any muscular tension* allowing it to soften as you breathe out.

Setting aside time to practise mindfulness on a daily basis, even for just ten minutes at a time, incorporating it regularly into your daily life, will train you to become increasingly present and accepting of your experiences, whatever they are, without trying to resist or push them away if they feel unpleasant, without attempting to hold onto them if they are enjoyable.

During your practice you are not trying to achieve any end goal or any particular state of mind or feeling. There is no right or wrong. You are simply appreciating each moment for what it is. There's nothing magical or mystical about mindfulness. It's important not to complicate things and miss out on the simplicity of the experience. The present moment is somewhere you have always been, therefore it's a completely familiar place to be and easily overlooked. The idea is just to be aware of 'now' and keep bringing yourself back to this point.

Don't be put off when you get carried away by your thought- stream. It's perfectly normal. In fact, it's your awareness of this tendency to get caught up in thoughts that is enlightening, as you can see how much of the time your consciousness gets pulled away from where you are. Returning to the breath as an anchor during a mindful session is helpful; and since we breathe anyway it's an ever-present tool to use.

I have carefully chosen the quotations in this book that have the 'ring of truth' for me and I sincerely hope each one will enhance your understanding and appreciation of the nature of mindfulness. I have included the various aspects of mindfulness:-

- Awareness of the present moment
- Being non-judgemental
- Acceptance of things exactly as they are right now.
- Compassion

This last aspect encompasses *self-*compassion which is frequently neglected.

I sincerely hope that mindfulness will prove as exciting and enriching to you as it has to me and that it will make as massive a difference to your life as it has to mine.

Being mindful is generally natural in childhood. At that stage we experience life as it is happening through our senses. To illustrate this I would like to quote from my book: 'And This Is My Adopted Daughter' about an experience when I was seven years old:

The air is still, hot and salty. I'm alone but not lonely, happy to be sitting on the shingles outside our holiday bungalow, a short walk from the beach.

I run my fingers over the smooth, warm pebbles, their pale colours glowing in the sunlight. I look up, watching and listening to the seagulls flying overhead...

Now there is silence, except for crickets in the tufty grass. It's like they're singing just for me.

I feel safe here. Beyond the thin wire fencing of the garden, I see bright red poppies and yellow ragwort.

The smell of my favourite roast lunch makes me feel hungry. Mummy is calling me, but I don't want to move. I'm so comfortable. It's like I'm part of this garden. I feel happy and peaceful here.

I stopped typing a short while ago to go into the garden and sit on my patio. I was aware of the rise and fall of my belly as I breathed, became conscious of the tension in my shoulders and jaw slowly lessening.

The sun felt warm on my skin; I listened to the blackbird singing its song; watched the clouds drifting in a blue sky.

My thoughts strayed to this book; I returned my attention to my breathing.

The smell of apple blossom on the tree floated on the breeze towards me; I heard the sound of children's voices in the distance; noticed the sparrow hopping across the grass.

Now I've returned to my computer to write the final paragraphs of the introduction to this book.

'Moments of Mindfulness' is for you to dip into rather than read straight through, choosing a quotation at random to think about its meaning and relevance to your life. You can also mull over the subtle variations in the little flower drawing on each page.

Keeping it by your bedside will allow you to meditate on one before you sleep; you might also wish to pick a quote each morning to reflect on during the day.

However you use it - enjoy it, mindfully!

Tomorrow is not real. It is an illusion. The only reality is now.

Zen Master

If you want to conquer the anxiety of life, live in the moment, live in the breath.

Amit Ray

I got the blues thinking of the future, so I left off and made some marmalade. It's amazing how it cheers one up to shred oranges and scrub the floor.

D.H. Lawrence

You can't breathe in the future, or in the past. You can only breathe now. By concentrating on your breath, you will still your panic and the anxiety, which tends to make your breathing shallow and fast. Slow breathing helps you stay in the present, another word for a gift. Place one finger over your nostril: this will half the speed at which you breathe. By forcing you to breathe more slowly, in turn your body is forced to calm down, and with it your anxious racing mind. Treat the breath as your anchor. Your mind will wander, that's what minds do. But gently keep bringing your attention back to the breath.

Rachel Kelly

What lies behind us and what lies before us are tiny matters compared to what lies within us.

Ralph Waldo Emerson

The most powerful relationship
you will ever have is the
relationship with yourself.

Steve Maraboli

To be beautiful means to be yourself. You don't need to be accepted by others. You need to accept yourself.

Thich Nhat Hanh

Loving yourself...does not mean being self-absorbed or narcissistic, or disregarding others. Rather it means welcoming yourself as the most honored guest in your own heart, a guest worthy of respect, a lovable companion.

Margo Anand

Mindfulness is a state of active, open attention on the present. When you're mindful, you observe your thoughts and feelings from a distance, without judging them good or bad. Instead of letting your life pass you by, mindfulness means living in the moment and awakening to experience.

Psychology Today

Observe the space between your thoughts, then observe the observer.

Hamilton Boudreaux

Some people do not know the difference between mindfulness and concentration. They concentrate on what they're doing, thinking that is being mindful. . . . We can concentrate on what we are doing, but if we are not mindful at the same time, with the ability to reflect on the moment, then if somebody interferes with our concentration, we may blow up, get carried away by anger at being frustrated. If we are mindful, we are aware of the tendency to first concentrate and then to feel anger when something interferes with that concentration. With mindfulness we can concentrate when it is appropriate to do so and not concentrate when it is appropriate not to do so.

Ajahn Sumedho

Our suffering stems from ignorance. We react because we do not know what we are doing, because we do not know the reality of ourselves. The mind spends most of the time lost in fantasies and illusions, reliving pleasant or unpleasant experiences and anticipating the future with eagerness or fear. While lost in such cravings or aversions, we are unaware of what is happening now, what we are doing now. Yet surely this moment, now, is the most important for us. We cannot live in the past; it is gone. Nor can we live in the future; it is forever beyond our grasp. We can live only in the present. If we are unaware of our present actions, we are condemned to repeating the mistakes of the past and can never succeed in attaining our dreams for the future. But if we can develop the ability to be aware of the present moment, we can use the past as a guide for ordering our actions in the future, so that we may attain our goal.

S.N. Goenka

Living in the moment means letting go of the past and not waiting for the future. It means living your life consciously, aware that each moment you breathe is a gift.

Oprah Winfrey

When you become good at the art of letting sufferings go, then you'll come to realize what you were dragging around with you. And for that, no one else other than you was responsible.

Bhagwan Shree Rajneesh

Silence is the great teacher and to learn its lessons you must pay attention to it. There is no substitute for the creative inspiration, knowledge, and stability that come from knowing how to contact your core of inner silence.

Deepak Chopra

Begin doing what you want to do now. We are not living in eternity. We have only this moment, sparkling like a star in our hand- and melting like a snowflake.

Francis Bacon Sr

You can't keep saying and doing the same things and expect better results. When you see your behavior clearly you can frame new responses. There are many techniques for increasing self-awareness. Most involve mindfulness--observing what's happening in the present moment: your thoughts, emotions, and bodily sensations.

Joan Duncan Oliver

Cultivating a generous spirit starts with mindfulness. Mindfulness, simply stated, means paying attention to what is actually happening; it's about what is really going on.

Nell Newman

Mindfulness can be summed up in two words: pay attention. Once you notice what you're doing, you have the power to change it.

Michelle Burford

Do we ever question the need to brush our teeth? Or say, "today I do not have time for brushing teeth?" Can we go a week without brushing? What that would be like? Please imagine it right now. How will the mouth and teeth feel? Do we believe if we brush teeth we will never need a dentist? And how about putting in a comparable amount of time, energy and regular practice to keep the mind clear, fresh, and refreshed? Or regularly brushing and clearing the mind from harmful residue? I view Mindfulness as a way of maintaining mental hygiene the same way brushing is needed for dental hygiene. And, from time to time, we may even need professional help for best results.

Rezvan Ameli

Mindfulness is simply being aware of what is happening right now without wishing it were different; enjoying the pleasant without holding on when it changes (which it will); being with the unpleasant without fearing it will always be this way (which it won't).

James Baraz

Mindfulness, also called wise attention, helps us see what we're adding to our experiences, not only during meditation sessions but also elsewhere.

Sharon Salzberg

In today's rush we all think too much, seek too much, want too much and forget about the joy of just being.

Eckhart Tolle

Feelings come and go like clouds in a windy sky. Conscious breathing is my anchor.

Thich Nhat Hanh

Suffering usually relates to wanting things to be different from the way they are.

Allan Lokos

If we learn to open our hearts, anyone, including the people who drive us crazy, can be our teacher.

Pema Chodron

Mindfulness takes a lot of work, but the good news is that the longer you practice, the easier it gets, and the more joyful your life becomes. At first, your thoughts will be in chaos, and everything will seem out of control. Your situation will feel helpless, but the more you focus on being fully where you are, the easier it will be to find peace of mind in the moment.

Henri Junttila

The present moment is never intolerable. What's intolerable is what's going to happen in the next four hours. To have your body here at 8 pm and your mind at 10:30 pm, that's what causes us suffering.

Anthony de Mello

The more I give myself permission to live in the moment and enjoy it without feeling guilty . . . the better I feel about the quality of my work.

Wayne Dyer

The ability to be in the present moment is a major component of mental wellness.

Abraham Maslow

The secret of health for both mind and body is not to mourn for the past, worry about the future, or anticipate troubles, but to live in the present moment wisely and earnestly.

Buddha

The past is a ghost, the future a dream. All we ever have is now.

Bill Cosby

Let us not look back in anger, nor forward in fear, but around in awareness.

James Thurber

There will be times when you attach to things and situations that you want, which will make it difficult to be fully in the present moment. It's impossible to be mindful when you're dwelling on the past or obsessing about the future. We all do those things sometimes. I've experienced it countless times in my own life. The more I want something, the more I fixate on not having it and wanting to get it. Once I release the attachment and focus on being grateful for what I have in the moment, my life seems to shift, and progress seems to happen naturally.

Henri Junttila

There are fine things which you mean to do some day, under what you think will be more favorable circumstances. But the only time that is surely yours is the present.

Grenville Kleise

Unease, anxiety, tension, stress, worry — all forms of fear — are caused by too much future, and not enough presence. Guilt, regret, resentment, grievances, sadness, bitterness, and all forms of nonforgiveness are caused by too much past, and not enough presence.

Eckhart Tolle

Mindfulness meditation should be more than just watching what you are doing. What you really need to watch is your motivation.

Lama Zopa Rinpoche

Mindfulness develops attention, concentration and the ability to simply be present with little or no future orientation, past orientation or goal orientation—choosing to be a human being rather than a human doing.

Ian Gawler, Paul Bedson

The goal of mindfulness is to become fully aware of the thoughts one is having, and of the emotions one is experiencing.

Larry Shapiro

Mindfulness gives you time. Time gives you choices. Choices, skillfully made, lead to freedom. You don't have to be swept away by your feeling. You can respond with wisdom and kindness rather than habit and reactivity.

Bhante Henepola Gunaratana

When we let go of wanting something else to happen in this moment, we are taking a profound step toward being able to encounter what is here now. If we hope to go anywhere or develop ourselves in any way, we can only step from where we are standing. If we don't really know where we are standing—a knowing that comes directly from the cultivation of mindfulness—we may only go in circles, for all our efforts and expectations. So, in meditation practice, the best way to get somewhere is to let go of trying to get anywhere at all.

Jon Kabat-Zinn

Mindfulness helps us get better at seeing the difference between what's happening and the stories we tell ourselves about what's happening, stories that get in the way of direct experience. Often such stories treat a fleeting state of mind as if it were our entire and permanent self.

Sharon Salzberg

Mindfulness and compassion actually develop at the same pace. The more mindful you become, the easier you'll find it to be compassionate. And the more you open your heart to others, the more mindful you become in all your activities.

Mingyur Rinpoche

Don't believe everything you think.
Thoughts are just that - thoughts.

Allan Lokos

When we feel compassion for others, we feel kindness toward them, empathy, and a desire to help reduce their suffering. It's the same when you are compassionate toward yourself. Self-compassion creates a caring space within you that is free of judgment—a place that sees your hurt and your failures and softens to allow those experiences with kindness and caring.

Bobbi Emel

Be gentle first with yourself if you wish to be gentle with others.

Lama Yeshe

Mindful self-compassion can be learned by anyone. It's the practice of repeatedly evoking good will toward ourselves especially when we're suffering — cultivating the same desire that all living beings have to live happily and free from suffering.

Christopher Germer

Acceptance of one's life has nothing to do with resignation; it does not mean running away from the struggle. On the contrary, it means accepting it as it comes, with all the handicaps of heredity, of suffering, of psychological complexes and injustices.

Paul Tournier

The first step toward change is awareness. The second step is acceptance.

Nathaniel Branden

Mindfulness is a state that can be cultivated in which one is acutely aware of one's present experience and responds to this experience in a non-judgmental and non-reactive way. The practice of mindfulness often leads to a sense of balance and psychological well-being.

Carmody & Baer

To cultivate mindfulness a person does not try to create any particular state of mind, but attempts to just become aware of each thought, feeling, or sensation as it arises in the present moment and to let each thought, sensation, or feeling pass away without judgment or attachment . While this is a simple practice, it can be both challenging and transformative.

Segal, Williams, & Teasdale

You shouldn't chase after the past, or place expectations on the future. What is past is left behind. The future is as yet unreached. Whatever quality is present you clearly see right there.

Thanissaro Bhikkhu

When we put down ideas of what life should be like, we are free to wholeheartedly say yes to our life as it is

Tara Brach

Every religious tradition describes the 'still, small voice within' that speaks clearly but quietly. When we listen to our inner wisdom, we tend to choose foods and ways of living that are more healthful.

Dean Ornish

The passing moment is all that we can be sure of; it is only common sense to extract its utmost value from it.

W. Somerset Maugham

Slow down and enjoy life. It's not only the scenery you miss by going too fast – you also miss the sense of where you are going and why.

Eddie Cantor

As you walk and eat and travel, be where you are. Otherwise you will miss most of your life.

Buddha

The way to live in the present is to remember that "This too shall pass." When you experience joy, remembering that "This too shall pass" helps you savor the here and now. When you experience pain and sorrow, remembering that "This too shall pass" reminds you that grief, like joy, is only temporary.

Joey Green

Human beings, by changing the inner attitudes of their minds, can change the outer aspects of their lives.

William James

71

How we spend our days is of course how we spend our lives.

Anne Dillard

If you worry about what might be, and wonder what might have been, you will ignore what is.

Unknown

Practicing mindfulness means we practice our awareness in all our actions. Whether we are washing dishes or tying our shoes, our mind is focused on whatever we are doing. We are not thinking about the bills that we have to pay, or the phone call we need to make when we get to the office. We are simply living in the moment.

Jonathan (blogger)

Life is all memory, except for the one present moment that goes by you so quickly you hardly catch it going.

Tennessee Williams

This moment is the moment of reality, of union, of truth. Nothing needs to be done to it or to you for this to be so. Nothing needs to be avoided, transcended, or found for it to be so.

Da Avabhasa

Being present begins with NOTICING when we are trying to alter the present moment. To be present, we must first accept it. This is known as the Paradoxical Theory of Change.

John Kuypers

Each second we live is a new and unique moment of the universe, a moment that never was before and never will be again.

Pau Casals

I realized that living in the present is not an idea. It's reality. It's like taking one step at a time. Sounds good. Good philosophy, right? Then it occurred to me, Have you ever taken two steps at a time? We can't. It's as simple as that: we can't. It's the same with living in the present. Our thoughts may wander to the past or the future. Yet, our thoughts are just thoughts. Our bodies are in the present. We are in the present. That's just the way it is.

Anne Wilson Schaef

If we know that we are now at the point where we have always wanted to be, we will be there. . . because we are never there but always here, now!

Paul Twitchell

Live in the present. Do the things that need to be done. Do all the good you can each day. The future will unfold.

Peace Pilgrim

Don't think about the future. Just be here now. Don't think about the past. Just be here now.

Ram Dass

Not living in the present is a form of denial. It's easier to live in the past or future because then you don't have to be responsible for the present.

Jane Hendrix

We hurry through the so-called boring things in order to attend to that which we deem more important, interesting. Perhaps the final freedom will be a recognition that everything in every moment is 'essential' and that nothing at all is 'important.'

Helen M. Luke

The ability to live fully in the moment-- in the time and place we are right now-- is one of the greatest secrets I know of living joyfully. Because once you grasp it, freedom is very close. You stop worrying about the past and stressing out about the future. Enjoying life--not agonizing about what happened yesterday or what might happen tomorrow--becomes your priority. Your days become a gift, not a grind.

Patti LaBelle

People who are "being" are fully present. They are totally engaged in the moment. This engagement includes an easy appreciation and sense of connection with whomever or whatever they are relating to at the time. These people are aware of a job well done or a difficulty surmounted and will respect and often acknowledge the person who has accomplished it. "Being" is a state of heart and mind that is receptive and able to listen carefully.

Sallirae Henderson

The future is always
beginning now.

Mark Strand

We're so busy watching out for what's just ahead of us that we don't take time to enjoy where we are.

Bill Watterson

M - *Moment-to-moment attention*

I - *In the here-and-now*

N - *Non-judgmental attitude*

D - *Detach from unhelpful thoughts*

F - *Forgive & be grateful*

U - *Unconditional acceptance*

L - *Learn with beginner's mind*

Zhen-Phang

Mindfulness means being aware of how you're deploying your attention and making decisions about it, and not letting the tweet or the buzzing of your BlackBerry call your attention.

Howard Rheingold

Mindfulness helps us freeze the frame so that we can become aware of our sensations and experiences as they are, without the distorting coloration of socially conditioned responses or habitual reactions.

Henepola Gunaratana

Be mindful of what you say when you talk to yourself.

Duane Morse

Tell me to what you pay attention and I will tell you who you are.

Jose Ortega y Gasset

There are two days in a year in which nothing can be done: "yesterday" and "tomorrow."

Anon

All the elements for your happiness are already here. There's no need to run, strive, search or struggle. Just be.

Jon Kabat-Zinn

While it may be difficult to change the world, it is always possible to change the way we look at it.

Matthieu Ricard

Mindfulness is the aware, balanced acceptance of the present experience. It isn't more complicated than that. It is opening to or receiving the present moment, pleasant or unpleasant, just as it is, without either clinging to it or rejecting it.

Sylvia Boorstein

Try pausing right before and right after undertaking a new action, even something simple like putting a key in a lock to open a door. Such pauses take a brief moment, yet they have the effect of decompressing time and centering you.

David Steindl-Rast

In the space between your thoughts there is your truth.

Reuben Lowe

Life is a great and wondrous mystery, and the only thing we know that we have for sure is what is right here and right now. Don't miss it.

Leo Buscaglia

Since my house burned down I now own a better view of the rising moon.

Mizuta Masahide

It's being here now that's important. There's no past and there's no future. Time is a very misleading thing. All there is ever, is the now. We can gain experience from the past, but we can't relive it; and we can hope for the future, but we don't know if there is one.

George Harrison

For many years, at great cost, I traveled through many countries, saw the high mountains, the oceans. The only things I did not see were the sparkling dewdrops in the grass just outside my door.

Rabindranath Tagore

When we are in the midst of chaos, let go of the need to control it. Be awash in it, experience it in that moment, try not to control the outcome but deal with the flow as it comes.

Leo Babauta

We see things not as they are, but as we are.

H. M. Tomlinson

Somewhere in this process you will come face-to-face with the sudden and shocking realization that you are completely crazy. Your mind is a shrieking gibbering madhouse on wheels barreling pell-mell down the hill utterly out of control and helpless. No problem. You are not crazier than you were yesterday. It has always been this way and you just never noticed. You are also no crazier than everyone else around you. The only real difference is that you have confronted the situation they have not.

Henepola Gunaratana

Bring your attention to your natural breathing process. Locate the area where the breath is most clear and let awareness lightly rest there. For some it is the sensation of the rising and falling of the abdomen. For others it may be the sensations experienced at the nostrils with the inhalation and exhalation. You can use very soft mental labels to guide and sustain attention to the breath. "Rising/falling" for the abdomen and "in/out" for the nostrils. Let the breath breathe itself without control, direction, or force. Feel each breath from within the breath, not from the head. Feel the full breath cycle from the beginning through the middle to the end.

Steven Smith

Breath a an anchor imply
mean that when we begin to it
till, we can u e our focu ed
attention to our breath a a ignal
to the mind/body that it i time to
be fully pre ent. A your mind
wander , don t be di couraged,
ju t gently bring your elf back to
the breath.

Jennifer Roberts

Mindfulness is an emotionally non-reactive state. We don't judge that this experience is good and that one is bad. Or if we do make those judgments we simply notice them and let go of them.

Bodhipaksa

In some ways mindfulness is incredibly simple. It has been defined as awareness of present moment experience with acceptance and kindness. The learning of mindfulness often involves a structured practice where one focuses on the breath as an anchor to the present moment, and allows thoughts, feelings, and body sensations to arise, whilst staying with the breath.

Dan Entmacher

Mindfulness is being aware of yourself, others, and your surroundings in the moment. When consciously and kindly focusing awareness on life as it unfolds minute by precious minute, you are better able to savor each experience. Also, being closely attentive gives you the opportunity to change unwise or painful feelings and responses quickly. In fact, being truly present in a mindful way is an excellent stress reducer and, because of that, can be seen as consciousness conditioning, a strengthening workout for body, mind, heart, and spirit.

Sue Patton Thoele

Two thoughts cannot coexist at the same time: if the clear light of mindfulness is present, there is no room for mental twilight.

Nyanaponika Thera

When we stop trying to force pleasant feelings, they are freer to emerge on their own.

When we stop trying to resist unpleasant feelings, we may find that they can drift away by themselves.

When we stop trying to make something happen, a whole world of fresh and unanticipated experiences may become accessible to us.

Mark Williams

113

Mindfulness demists the windscreen of our perception.

Polly Fielding

6451214R00067

Printed in Great Britain
by Amazon.co.uk, Ltd.,
Marston Gate.